# life/slices

FLOWERSONG
PRESS

poems by

## Gene Novogrodsky

FlowerSong Press
Copyright © 2021 by Eugene "Gene" Novogrodsky
ISBN: 978-1-953447-74-6
Library of Congress Number: 2021940705

Published by FlowerSong Press
in the United States of America.
www.flowersongpress.com

Cover art: "Los días oscuros" 262
by Octavio quintanilla
IG: @writeroctavioquintanilla

Cover Design by Priscilla Celina Suarez
Set in Adobe Garamond Pro

# life /slices

by Gene Novogrodsky

# ACKNOWLEDGEMENTS

"Writing"
"Train Talk"
"Brief"

originally appeared in the *San Antonio Express-News*

More than a decade of Gene Novogrodsky's work
(many included in this volume)

appeared in posts on the site Writers of the Rio Grande

"Somewhere Along the Borderline" by Glen Sorestad

originally appeared in *The Malpais Review*,
Vol. 6, No. 1, 2015

"Afternoon of Gifts"
"Rambling Stories"        by Chip Dameron

originally appeared in *Waiting for an Etcher*,
Lamar University Press, 2015

# DEDICATION

A long over-due thanks to Nancy Ruth Slate Mires and Ruth Elizabeth Wagner for decades of support as I worked on my slices; their patience was, and is, remarkable. And a thanks, too, to the Barre Montpelier Times Argus editors, especially Tom Sivert, for helping me approach succinctness. Finally, a thank you to all in the Narcisco Martinez Cultural Arts Center Writers Forum in San Benito and those in various ad hoc writing groups in Brownsville who have listened to me read for hours.

# TABLE OF CONTENTS


*Political*

Border Virus Slice......4

Right Now......6

Waiting......7

She Says......8

To Work......9

Train Talk......10

Border Lines, Brief......11

Freedom......13

The Art Opening......14

Number(s)......17

Those Arms......18

Wedding, But......19

Color, Ever Color......20

*Baseball*

Spikes......24

A Mother's Mind......25

Out of the Game......27

Wrigley Field, and I Walk Away......28

Fields......30

Rained Out......31

Deliveries......34
Curl to Sleep......35
Signs......36
Pitchers and Catchers Report......38
Final Out......39
Due Up......40
...An Arizona End......41
Retain......44
Early Baseball......45

## Stories

Cilantro......50
Jumble......51
Wood......52
Brief......53
The Mailman......54
White Girl......55
To Drive......57
Picking......58
Stand Your Ground......59
Ox Man......62
Arkansas/Texas Pimpled Girl......64
Red Smudges......66
Sisters......67
On Rises......68
Start......69
Blood and Tribes......70
Blanket......71

## The Run of Days

Straight Tie......76
Through Flowers......77

Up and Down the Hilly Road......78

Daylight Savings Ends......79

Dormancy......80

Sound Of Silence......82

Couch......83

I Did......85

Limping......86

Another Day, Hour......87

Fog Movement......89

Two Grapefruit......90

Lying There......91

*Epiphanies*

Wild Olive White......96

And Now......97

The Poets See......98

Same Planet (Slight Variations)......99

Downtown In Late April......100

Alley......103

Tears, Unexplained......104

Independence......108

Unwelcoming Prudence......109

Ineptitude Slotted......110

To Seed......111

Orange In the West......112

Smell......113

Crow Feather......114

Vulnerability......115

*For Gene*

Gene's Last Game......120

Somewhere Along the Border Line......121

Poem for Miriam Rodriguez......122
Afternoon of Gifts......123
Last Mail Run......124
Mr. Novo......125
Rambling Stories......126
Somewhere in Maine......128
End of the Rio Grande......129
December Walk with Gene......130

*Political*

Gene's political poems are about place, a particular place—the South Texas Borderlands—and to write about this place the way Gene Novogrodsky does, one has to have lived here. You can't bullshit this sort of intimate knowledge of the Borderlands without having lived here. And Gene has lived in South Texas for innumerable years. He breathes border and sometimes his breath reaches deeper south to Guadalajara. He discerns hope and despair from a distance with an eagle's eye and then paints a slice of daily life with words, without judgment. He illuminates lives that often go unseen and unheard, lives that, despite hardship, remain unbroken. What attracts me to these poems is Gene's deep sense of empathy, an empathy of one who has crossed unfamiliar borders and lived to tell the story. There is no pretense here, only the truth of a poet-elder, a Borderland sage documenting the people, the struggle, the dream. After all, the heart of these poems is made of dreams—dreams of a better job, a better life; dreams of a new beginning amiable to human dignity.

**Octavio Quintanilla**

## Border Virus Slice

...with dawn gone to muted light,

The border city quietly stirs.

Bridge crossers, scant in number,

Line to sell plasma;

They step over and around huddled homeless.

A woman looks for a lost kitty.

"I saved it yesterday.

"It hopped out of my car downtown.

"Now I leave food out, trying to lure it back."

Four Sri Lankans walk around and around the block.

They'd spent five months in the federal detention facility,

Got asylum, and now were waiting for a friend to drive them to New York for restaurant work.

"We flew from Sri Lanka to Dubai to Moscow to Panama City.

"We walked eight days through the jungle,

"And then got buses through Central America and Mexico to Reynosa.

"We had a good lawyer and that helped us get asylum."

They were too young to recall Sri Lanka's civil war.

They, by the way, the losing side: Tamil they were..


Some of the homeless were up,

Adjusting their bedrolls, clothes and cardboard.

The kitten seeker went around and around, no kitten.

The Sri Lankans' ride came, and they left,

Valuable asylum acceptance papers in hand.

More plasma sellers lined up.

Rare vehicles entering the United States,

Construction workers and providers.

More on foot, though.

A hazy sun broke through the clouds ....


[mid April on the border, 2020, time of the virus]

# Right Now

Global reach.

Prices jump, higher, higher.

If you're fortunate enough to live within a kilometer of prosperity,

Beyond the global claws, fangs and teeth,

You walk right in, carrying a bucket, rag and soap,

Ready to scrub cars and trucks.

And you might also walk right in,

Ready to do anything, yes, anything ....

Tacos, sodas, a half liter of fuel back home, cash ....

Warding off those global arms ....

[mid January 2017]

## Waiting

....rain, heavy, in Matamoros;

Migrants, waiting and waiting some more,

Ever waiting ....

In their wind-rain-on-top tents ...

None outdoors ....

From the tents, voices subdued within ....

Three men walk among bridge-in-line cars,

Windshield wipers they sell,

Good business ...

Then, a soldier approaches, wanting his cut ....

The wiper vendors move away - fast.

Deeper in the city, jammed sidewalks, holiday buying.

Car lights on at twilight at the bridge.

Wet, so wet, puddles, drops strong ....

And tent voices meld, muffle ....


[date unknown]

## She Says

She takes a laundromat cigarette break with a hot orange sun rising
behind her

"Once a week I do the laundry.

"I like to sit here and have an early morning smoke."

Now, think about her:

Years as a migrant, born in a remote Texas county in the midst of hand-
picked cotton time.

Then, beets and fruit from Nebraska to Utah.

"After that, 30 years of housekeeping in a hospital.

"Without us, infections."

There, right to the point,

And it applied years ago, and now in virus time:

Those who get the food ….

Those who scrub the floors ….

Millions.

Where are they when not bending lifting doing …?

"Got to get back.

"The clothes are dry."

From me, a thanks to her,

And the words fail to declare my awe, appreciation and privilege ….

[mid May 2020]

## To Work

Why do they come?

What's happening down there,

Mexico and Central America?

Leave that to the economists,

Political scientists ....

All I know is what I saw in early May:

Ninety-two men and women from Chiapas and Yucatan,

Seventy-six men and women from Oaxaca and Veracruz,

Pushing and pulling suitcases across the international bridge between
Matamoros and Brownsville,

All with papers in order,

The first group off to north Texas for six months of carnival work,

The other off to southern Louisiana for five months of crab packing,

Tents up, tents down, rides up, rides down,

Blue legs, bodies into cans ....

I'd tell those book-writing experts one thing:

Go stand on the international bridge, and ask some questions.

Your studies will improve.

[late May 2014]

## Train Talk

To regard Mississippi: Death.

Dead Emmett Till.

Dead Michael Schwerner.

Dead Andrew Goodman.

Dead James Chaney.

The Amtrak - slow its speed

Moves across southeast Mississippi,

Pines, soybean fields, swamps ... blur ....

Across the aisle, a black woman,

Home, Meridian and Philadelphia, Mississippi.

I mention Emmett Till, then Schwerner, Goodman and Chaney.

"Oh, I lived two blocks from James."

I cry, wet tears onto my cheeks.

She doesn't.

[Summer 2018]

## Border Lines, Brief

…"four-person business in Houston, rich people's yards, now off to Tampico for our twice yearly family visit; we're not afraid of the six or more hours.

Pick-up packed, pesos obtained …off it roars ….

…"no papers, my kids have them, born here, I stay low, and do not break laws, selling used clothing."

Rushes into public housing, fast, hunched.

…"cancer, many operations, at least I have government help."

And various prison jobs with youth, maybe to resume.

…"hey, pull my ATM card out; my finger nails are too long; this baby in me will be number three."

Plasma given, money on card, a mother to be, again.

…"from Florida to Robstown, Texas, and now with my mom in Reynosa; I'd been to Matamoros to see a cousin; the beach idea fell apart, matter of papers. Stay with me until my bus to McAllen comes."

So many bags, but 19 young years, and maybe some school interest, for now, work in stores like her mother.

…"waiting I am for the South Padre bus, housekeeping work, a lot of back and forth; sometimes I get a ride."

Cheerful waiting for the bus, no gloom over making beds, sweeping, changing towels.

…"nothing to do, nothing."

Hold it together, pedal on, motorcycle on, drive on, and wait for TV sports to return.

…"pleased to do this prayer from curbside."

Two in a car, windows down, masks on, look to the kneeling masked priest.

…"it is only a question of 'where and when.'"

Yes, that is real, very real.

***

Yes, in the time-of-virus, the façade is ripped, revealing what has long been there ….

Did I need to say that?

Yes, I did, checking the don't-forget box!

[late May 2020]

**Freedom**

TV cars ads promise freedom.

Just buy and drive.

Selling ( omitting ) indebtedness and confinement.

[mid July 2015]

## The Art Opening

I tell the four-time Iraq War vet, a sometimes shaky man,

That I was angry at the art opening.

About 100 viewers, stepping close to the paintings,

Stepping back from them.

Serious observers.

The women, heels, perfume, new dresses, skirts,

The men, fresh haircuts, new shirts, pressed slacks,

Comfortable twilight for art:

Shrimp, cold cuts, cookies on  tables,

Wine on side tables,

Upstairs and downstairs,

A grassy center of the brick building,

Varnished stairs, floors.

Live music.

Of the 100, I knew  that five - at the most -

Had done anything publicly to oppose the war,

The war on its tenth anniversary -

Same date as the art show.

----

They'd gone to the same art shows,

Same concerts,

Same meals,

And the war continued,

Thousands of dead Iraqis and Americans,

Many thousands more wounded,

And uncounted ones, like the vet,

Left shaky, or much worse ....

---

The vet listened.

He wasn't surprised.

"I've seen all that, all  the time.

I don't get mad like you."

---

I tell him:

"Look at the war, for oil, for defense contractors,

For nothing, men sent, even if volunteers, horrible."

---

He repeats,

"Relax, relax."

---

But the smugness, smugness.

I walk home, walking it off.

Now night ....

[late March 2013]

# Number(s)

The federal Bureau Of Prisons' website, attractive,

What with flowers sprinkling the inmate locator information ....

The state sites are also mellow .....

Not a hint of the millions confined, often in solitary .....

Not a hint of the unexplained transfers ....

Type in the number, get the release date, get the current prison ....

How clean, efficient,

How removed ....

2019, 2059,

Mere numbers ....

[late January 2018]

## Those Arms

Parents hold the babies;

The babies grow, leave, seek space, often deep.

The maids and nannies,

Brown, black, white, mixed-hue arms hold the babies;

The babies grow, leave, seek space, and forget.

"I held her four full months,

Then watched her for years.

I never see her anymore," a maid reflects.

Arms, so occupied, so heavy,

Now free, and all move, remember infrequently ....

[late February 2016]

## Wedding, But

Say it before you flip to anger: The posh wedding in Guadalajara was a celebration of hope;

May the couple prosper and act decently and fairly to all...

OK, that said, my knowledge of history kicked in:

Guadalajara and Jalisco State, new cartels kill and try to fill vacuums....

Hundreds of thousands short dark Huicholes from the bluish mountains clean, sweep, polish, lift ....

White Guadalajara's millions continue; new-car dealerships. hundreds of thousands tourists, restaurants, hotels ....

Several thousand central Americans to the south wend north, only hours south ....

And to the north, the 43 dead students disintegrate to dust ....

Back to the wedding, a 400 year old cathedral,

So tall ...and the Huicholes who died on the trembling scaffolds ....

Surrounding haciendas, with vestiges of their bent Huichole workers ....

Now posh party sites, removed from the valley slums ....

Finally, Jalisco, site of the fascistic Cristo War against Mexico's secular government,

The Church trying to halt the Revolution of decades before ....

That is that; fine wedding and painful past and present ....

Ahistoric I am not ...by no means ....

[mid autumn 2018]

## Color, Ever Color

The soft brown.

Black eyes.

The chocolate brown.

Blacker eyes.

How you walked North America's spine.

Now, the blend with those who sailed the Atlantic's rise and fall.

[late December 2016]

# Baseball

◊◊◊◊◊◊◊◊◊◊◊◊◊◊◊◊◊◊◊

there is a well of nostalgia you can fall into when you write
about baseball. gene doesn't. sure, when we talk it - two old guys
jawing about days and players and games long past, we almost
drown in that well. but in his poems about the game he loves
there's none of that. there's all the joy, youth, exuberance, geometry,
place, names, particulars, the politics and the poetics of it –
gloriously personal and universal.

gene's baseball poems are stories and politics, dailiness, and
epiphanies, rich in the everyday joys of a game on a diamond.
and if there is any golden haze about the days and games and times
these poems describe, it is because those days were just exactly that
color, truth be told, and you need to know.

**JIM LAVILLA-HAVELIN**

**Spikes**

The spikes that often nicked my inside ankles

Are still in the house.

Fifty years plus since worn on semi-pro central Vermont baseball fields.

A touch of mold, faded polish, rusted iron ....

To bite into dirt, to bite into grass ....

[mid March 2019]

## A Mother's Mind

Parents' minds.

Do we know them?

Did we know them?

My mother, and those parts gone,

Never known,

Somewhere inside,

Cried but four times:

FDR's spring death.

Her father's spring death.

Babe Ruth's summer death.

Lou Gehrig's summer death, too.

I'd be playing ball,

I'd be coming home from the one-room school,

And there, was my mother, unknown then, unknown now, crying.

Sometimes I asked, sometimes I didn't, why ....

***

And decades before,

When an uncle I never knew, - her brother -

Ran across a New York City street,

And was killed by a car,

An early pedestrian/vehicle death,

(Record that!)

My mother saw him die on that bus and trolley and car and vehicle and vendors-filled street.

She must have cried then ....


[mid July 2015]

## Out of the Game

Will I be able to walk off off the
Field when a slow roller gets past me
And stops in soft grass in short right field?

Will I motion to the red-faced and paunchy
Manager glowering at me from the
Dugout steps that he needs to put Jimmy in,
Jimmy from the far corner of the bench?

Or, will the manager call time, walk out
With Jimmy, the kid, and tell me that I am done?

All in the top of the third inning,
The third inning ....

[Date unknown]

## Wrigley Field, and I Walk Away

I wasn't sad.

I merely was.

I wound my way down Wrigley Field's twisting walkways to the street.

My pencil-completed scorecard in backpack.

Ernie Banks' statue to side.

I joined the flow to the Red Line Elevated.

I had seen my last Major League game.

Wrigley Field, the lone holdout against lights, now has had them for years.

Bad enough.

Baseball is sun.

But a video scoreboard is on its way for 2014.

A modern distraction, a 21st Century eyesore, welcomed by millions.

Baseball games should be a treasured hours:

Games scored on paper.

Miss a play, that's it, no obtrusive screen in centerfield to show, tell, inform, announce.

Bad enough cellphones at games, little enough attention, soon less.

The crowd moved me up the passenger station steps.

My last Major League game was in my scorecard, Phillies' win over the

Cubs.

A fine afternoon, even as an ending.



[mid September 2013]

## Fields

...go to a game to see players,

Sit for the final play.

As for me,

The field,

Its green,

Reddish infield,

White bases,

Blue umpires ....

Before players,

Before the start ....

So beginnings,

The before ....

Appealing,

Then  uncertainty ....

[late summer]

## Rained Out

A neighbor coach, once a player, told me he wrote an essay that said,

"'No game today, rain!"

He received an A, and a warning not to try that lazy, if creative gimmick, again.

Rain blew in and down from settled clouds atop the Sierra Madre Oriental in Monclova, Mexico.

The white-blue uniformed Acereros of Monclova were supposed to play the orange-uniformed Leones of Yucatan.

Mexican Summer League, and come fall, Mexican Winter League.

They would manage only two plus innings in two damp twilights and nights.

Before the game: some running, catch and the magic of "pepper," soft bat, soft hands ....

Players at ease; players loosening.

Two steel mills beyond the outfield lights and ad-loaded fences and walls discharged gray smoke that met fog haze and rain.

Relax.

Sit.

I read that we Americans are watch watchers,

While Latinos are participants in and of time ....

Look at rich green grass, red infield dirt.

Look at the blue tarp handlers - pulling the billowing canvas over the already soaked grass and dirt.


Acereros visited with Leones, friends in the ancient league.

My dad introduced me to baseball in the 1946 Cards - Red Sox World Series.

Cards won.

He won money.

He was always a  National League fan.

I want to be an Acerero,

I want to be a Leon ....

To float off in a seat to baseball parks, fields ....

To be one with baseball ....

The rain pours.

The mountains disappear in smoke haze clouds rain.

The tarp becomes a gigantic swimming pool, if shallow.

I walk in water-over-my-shoes out of the parking lot, look for a cab.

Hard for drivers to find riders in the dark rain.

A stadium guard uses his yellow illuminated baton to nab a cab.

Down down into the flooded city.

I try again - next day - and this time take a bus filled with steel mill and rail-car manufacturing workers to the park in hills high.

The sun shines - doubleheader scheduled.

I settle, having mulled more watches and time.

No tarp, grass a deep green, rich red dirt,

Players running, playing catch, and ”pepper’s” crisp pace ....

I look up - and within five minutes, off the peaks gray-layered clouds
mound -

And the rain begins, and the tarp-men start unrolling, covering ....

The Acereos and Leones disappear  into their deep dugouts,

And the doubleheader is called off in a quarter hour ....

Winding walkway down, out of the ballpark, out of the puddled parking
lot,

To another bus, other fans walking with me ....

Watches and time, watches and time ....

The Leones’ team bus, with a huge painted orange lion on each side,
passes me ... to the team hotel ....

The Acereros drive their cars home ....

The bus, like the cab the night before, down down to the flooded low
city center ....

[late June 2014]

## Deliveries

At 85, no more hitter-stopping fastballs and curves.

"I never had a change-up, and no sliders then."

He finds roof and tree shade most of the hot year.

He finds sun on rare cool days.

Three younger generations visit.

Talking.

Eating.

He sits, stares,

Sometimes picks up the conversation.

But it's football, not baseball ....

Baseball, the 50s,

Yes, the 50s ....

So he turns back,

Sees a hitter flail,

Strike three ....

[late January 2019]

## Curl to Sleep

Chilly rain.

Damp night.

Rain like popcorn on the roof.

I curl under blankets,

And listen to baseball from Fenway,

Yankees at Red Sox.

Drizzle there.

Falling asleep.

The inning?

The score?

Sleep, and the popcorn uneven splats.

[late August 2017]

## Signs

Willie Mays stumbled out of the batter's box in his last year.

He then fell on a cold chalk line.

Robert Frost mumbled lines at JFK's inauguration.

He didn't try to finish the poem on a frigid day.

Elizabeth Taylor flubbed lines.

She turned from heavy to fat, no more major roles.

I turned, nudged my coffee cup and hot liquid spilled on me.

"No, we can clean it up. You stay there,"

Spoken at my lined face.

I looked up and the red and yellow engine was yards away.

I fell backwards.

The engineer blew a harsh whistle.

My pant's leg caught in the bike chain.

I fell forward:

Ripped left arm.

Cut lip.

Bruised right knee.

Bruised right wrist.

Sweets in hand broken on the street.

Had nearly fallen a day before.

Willie left baseball.

Frost went to his cabin, no more writing.

Taylor slumped into seclusion.

I check the coffee cup.

I get serious about stop, look, listen.

I fasten the helmet, check legs, focus ....

The signs are there ....

[late February 2013]

## Pitchers and Catchers Report

As January's cold folds into February's even colder days,

The news comes on:

"Pitchers and catchers will report to their camps next week."

I heard the words in 1947, and soon will hear them again.

Another year - as I mark my life - will begin.

The pitchers twisting to loosen.

The catchers lumbering under their masks, chest protectors, knee guards ....

White baseball in brown bags.

Coaches with clipboards.

Hurry to camp, pitchers and catchers.

Thanks for another year ....

And February will warm, after the cold's fierce visit ....

[late January 2019]

## Final Out

July's heat, mid-summer's visit,

Diminished green, parched fields ....

August would come, shorter and cooler days.

And I turn in my itchy gray red flannel baseball uniform

To the stocky player-manager.

I leave his driveway.

I see the stained green and brown canvas batting and ball bags in his garage.

He doesn't see my wet eyes.

He doesn't hear me mutter:

"Damn, too soon, I had more years, I was doing ok."

The final out.

If I said, "Wife, kids, no time,"

He'd shrug, spit, scratch a powerful forearm.

He wouldn't have a wife and kids hand him the final out.

No, not him, the longest player-manager in the Canadian Vermont New England Border League.

Never.

[early July 2014]

## Due Up

Uncle Dave was due up.

He played right field - a ninth player, if useless, needed to fill out the team.

No Uncle Dave showed at the feed-bag-serving-as-home-plate triangle.

Hitting and fielding teams looked out to the just-cut early summer pasture hill backed by a stone wall.

Uncle Dave was out there - asleep in the stubble, near cowshit piles.

The other team said he'd be declared an automatic out unless he came in within a minute.

If not, the next hitter would bat, one out recorded.

Uncle Dave slept on.

Three outs in a hurry.

No need for him to take his position.

He was there - asleep.

As for catching flies or fielding hits - no report from ninety years plus past of farm boy baseball in the hazy blue Catskills ....

[early May 2015]

## ...An Arizona End

...three days of twisting black buzzards,

Carrion seeking ,,,,

Branches bare below ....

The rot, the dead ....

***

And the two men just out of the Wisconsin State Prison stop.

"We're going to California, and you might need to drive."

"Fine; just say when."

The stop in southern Mississippi;

We go into a roadhouse;

They start sweet-talking the teen bar maid.

Smoke, juke box, sweat, kerosene ....

I'm nervous.

I edge to the door.

We leave to stares, and by central Louisiana I'm driving ....

...could have been bad, even worse....

No stop, into night, to day, to night, to day ....

A road blur.

They'd beaten two men with tire irons back in Wisconsin.

"They lived, though; we did time. But if they died, imagine."

On and on, across Texas ....

Jack rabbits into to the lights, bump, and flying lumps off to the dirt,
dead ....

Tumbleweed under the car, blown aside, off to the dirt ....

They sleep on;

Car seats, snug, no cells ....

Cool late winter to mild early spring ....

Arizona.

"Hey, thanks for the lift. Was glad to drive, But here I leave."

And I did, in Phoenix, where my father's Giants, now San Francisco,
were training ....

No matter, no New York ,,,but Giants ....

Their car heads west ....

Would they avoid more jail?

Desert cool to heat and sun ....

I'm dizzy, hungry, thirsty ....

And there I am, a thin fence from the Alou brothers: Jesus, Felipe and
Matty,

And Willie Mays .....

Catch they play.

Pepper they hit.

Now, I live for, "Pitchers and catchers to report early."

They must have arrived before my Arizona stop ....

...all players on the field, all ....

I'm tired, two days of drive, and the sun burns.

My father, a eight-year old, saw old Giants,

Close to his 200-apartment tenement ...

Now, his son trying to be American, sees them as 20-year old ....

My time by the fence, for him, for me ....

...no game today, just practice ...and where next ....?


[mid February 2018]

# Retain

To retain:

White pelicans, early spring,

Still in southern waters.

Baseball spike indentations

In home plate area's red clay.

[mid March 2016]

# Early Baseball

...and the rural carpenters/deer hunters, snow on plaid jackets, hand my dad $20, a lot of money in the cold and icy early fall of 1946.

...cigarettes/wood stoves/snow melt on floor/rural post office-store/and my dad's National League Cardinals had beaten their American League Red Sox.

...we drive home on ice and snow ....

...why December weather in October ...?

...my New York City father, the outsider, the stranger to guns, tobacco chewing, cigarettes, cursing ....

National League for my dad for more than 90 years ....

***

"I have two tickets from Dr. Cohen for the seventh game of the World Series (1947 Dodgers at Yankees)."

"Wow! I'm going with you."

"No, I'm taking your mother."

I scream.

"Please! Please!"

"You'll stay here and candle eggs; you can listen on the radio."

"My mother. She doesn't know a thing about baseball.

"I'll give her a question; if she misses I'll go."

"Go ahead, but you're not going; she is."

"Mom, what is a balk?" as she comes into the kitchen.

"I don't know, and I don't care. I'm going. You're not."

And I stay home, candle eggs and do not speak when my parents return at dark, the Yankees the winners, the game ending on a ground-ball double play.

More than 70 years later, I  know my mother liked getting off the farm, even it was to a baseball game ….

***

…in Miami 1950, and the Class B Miami Sun Sox are hosting the Lakeland Pilots in a Florida International League playoff game.

"I'm going," my father says.

"I'm going, too," I declare.

"No, you're not; you'll stay here with your mother and brother."

I cry, and get ready for sleep.

I'm asleep when my father comes back ….

…aware now, she did want a farm family break, but in 1950 she would have gone back in a day/never did ….

***

Baseball and Father and Mother.

Opera on radio in her bedroom.

Radio and TV in rest of the house, baseball for Father, Brother, me ….

Scores/standings/averages ….

Next Metropolitan Opera By Texaco for her ….

[late May 2020]

**Stories**

Stories, stories, and more stories. Some are family tales from long ago, some record his experiences on the road, some are rooted in Maine. Many come from conversations with the variety of folks he encounters in his daily outings in Brownsville, his hometown— counter clerk, midwife, sex worker, mailman, cancer patient. In stores, at the bus station, on the street, he listens, responds. He tells friends some of them, and many he retells as poetic slices. Whether rooted in his personal life or the lives of others, these poems take an unflinching look at being human.

CHIP DAMERON

## Cilantro (For Vanessa, a dear friend)

Green cilantro pokes from the brown bags.

Hot tortillas and greasy barbacoa deeper.

Sunday, and the customers line up,

Impatient, want to pay,

And return to running engines,

Families around tables,

Sunday established ....

A thin woman, in black,

Works the counter.

Her husband, and this was love,

Has died ....

The customers, impatient ....

[early May 2013]

## Jumble

...and my mother left South Florida's heat, with my brother,

For her childhood home in New York State's mountains ....

My father did wash, hung it out and then piled it on a bed.

We grabbed what we needed.

We ate seven nights a week in a downtown deli that had secure
parking ....

***

...and I walked, and thought my second shadow was another person;

No, it was me,

In the humid bath of South Texas ....

[mid-July 2015]

## Wood

She bends, gasps, throws wood chunks into her cellar.

Two old men, suspenders bursting, take a break - wood splitter cooling.

Two black crows settle on the road.

Nearer the cold, nearer ....

[early autumn 2018]

## Brief

He'd heard you pay more attention to the loon's call when death nears.

Yet, how would he have known the moment was so close?

He also laughed when his wife told him she was going to mow the cemetery in a drought.

She said there was enough grass to cut, and she did.

He woke at dawn, and went to the creaky wooden unpainted front porch.

He looked into the morning's damp fog.

He heard the loon down at the fog-covered pond.

He barely could see the red-rich apples on the tree atop the gray-blanketed meadow.

He walked back into the house, through the living room, time to turn on the coffee maker.

But his chest swelled between the rooms, he fell and died.

She slept through the thud.

Her cemetery mowing, up and down and around grave mounds, had tired her.

[Date unknown]

## The Mailman

Their mailman always advised:

"Keep you head on a swivel."

He'd learned that lesson in two long Iraqi tours.

Then, one day, a new mailman came, and then another.

They asked the substitutes about their regular mailman.

They missed his jaunty style.

Different explanations:

"Sick."

"Work injury."

"War stuff."

"PTSD."

The latter is heard the most.

Maybe he'll come back, maybe he won't.

The empire throws another stick in the pile ....

[mid February 2017]

## White Girl

I bang on the door.

"Yeah, wait," comes the voice.

I step back.

No windows, more a shed than an apartment.

I've read too many pistol-shot stories, but I'm still too close.

Two minutes pass in the hazy sun, wilted trees and lawn.

He finally looks around the door, white T-shirt over his belly, grey stubble on a lined face.

"C there?"

"No, the 'white girl,' right?"

"Yes."

"No, not here."

He slams the door.

I leave, and walk two blocks.

C is on a corner.

She's on her cellphone.

"What happened at your place?"

"Oh, the guy kept wanting me to buy him beer. I left, have a new place."

"Working the corners again?"

"Yeah, need to see the kids for the holidays. Two weeks in advance for a ticket gets it cheaper."

"No problem going to the North at the checkpoint?"

"No, none. I'm a white girl. I go right on through."

[late November 2012]

## To Drive

Three sisters and one ill mother,

Buying road tacos and coffee for the trip:

Three hundred plus miles to Houston and cancer treatment;

The sisters know the mother will get better,

She must get better.

A wet black road lines before them;

Into the car,

A sister drives, another next to her;

Two in the back with the dozing mother;

Treatments begin tomorrow,

For today is New Year's,

And what is another day?

Heat on in car,

Tacos and coffee strong ....

[early January 2020]

## Picking

Ruth in a shaky canoe.

She stretches for wild blueberries bending off a private, wooded island.

We skirted a wasps' gray white nest,

Brown wasps busy coming and going by the aperture,

The nest solidly formed like an Egyptian death mask.

Ruth has two hands on the scraggly berry bush.

I balance the canoe in a faint, lake chop.

A striped water snake slides off a mossy rock,

And swims curves under the canoe.

The berries?

Enough for a dozen muffins.


[late August 2019]

## Stand Your Ground

And I knew that northwest Florida was but an hour from Mobile.

And I thought Chet Garber lived over there, or he had the last time we spoke.

Why not!

My meeting was over; I had a new rental; the late afternoon had cooled, so off I drove to his small Florida town.

Crossman Street, that was it, Crossman Street, and I told that to the convenience store clerk.

Still plenty of sunlight.

"Two blocks ahead, then a left, and the 1300s should be there."

I got back in the rental, turned at Crossman and stopped in front of the 1344 that, I thought, was Chet's.

Again, sunlight, the blue Gulf just three streets south. I even saw the white waves.  Hot late afternoon, but a breeze from the gulf. Clouds fat, white, lifting.

I got out of the rental and started up 1344's walkway when I heard the shot.

My left arm burned and I saw blood.

"You're lucky I'm a bad shot," a voice from the stoop yelled.

"This is 'stand your ground' country you SOB!"

I was speechless.

In short seconds my arm had stopped bleeding, but it still burned.

I had not gotten to the door, but he must have seen me through a window from where he shot.

"Don't move! I'm calling the cops."

"This is crazy. I must have the wrong house."

"I don't know what the fuck you're talking about."

I heard the cops' sirens.

Soon, I'd be in the ER, and I hoped that I could drive there.

That's how I knew from movies the drill went: cops, then ER.

The rental had to be back tomorrow.

Where was Chet?

I was dizzy.

The shooter had come to stand over me, as I sat on his walkway.

Chet. So what. We hadn't spoken in years.

So impulsive this late afternoon.

Two cops now joined the shooter.

They stood over me.

"He was on my fuckin' property," the shooter said.

I could barely understand him.

Now, I heard ambulance sirens.

What a strange late-afternoon.

How long would the ER keep me?

Would I get the rental back by tomorrow?

Again, just where was Chet ...?

A streetlight came on, twilight ....

[early June 2019]

## Ox Man

The ox man died,

Whip on a barn wall,

Unintelligible New England ox commands gone.

A sour man, he found his moments when commanding his oxen,

Winning thousands at fairs,

Whip snapping,

Voice growling.

Fat stomach out of suspenders.

His wife lives,

A sweet woman:

"Take all the lettuce you want.

I live by forgetting and forgiving."

I break green leaves,

A week to go before seedy heads.

She smiles, bends for flowers and then starts to their home.

"Sorry about the beans," she yells back from a small porch.

"The deer got them, don't know why the dog didn't scare them."

Weeds circle his barn.

A tractor rusts.

The ox transport trailer's tires are flat.

The training circle weedy.

Concrete practice blocks weedy.

I turn the leaves into a sharp salad.

"Forget and forgive," decent advice ...

To attain such ....


[mid September 2013]

## Arkansas/Texas Pimpled Girl

Cat gray eyes.

Gritty light blonde hair.

Room rent due daily at noon -

If not, to the street ....

How to make the basic 40 dollars?

Two kids and a Mexican husband across.

"Met him in Arkansas.

"Trailer driver.

"Legal.

"Married him, my folks furious.

"Now for private reasons, I want a divorce.

"No, I won't say.

"He has the kids with his folks across.

"His mother is ok with the kids, bad with me.

"Yes, good Spanish I have, learned it from him.

"Did great in high school, dropped out in 10th grade,

"Math my only weak course.

"Angry at my folks, especially my abusive/drunk father.

"So I left home for good.

"He and his brothers don't work much across.

"Crime families all around them;

"They have a big house.

"My brother is in jail, no bail, on this side,

"Aggravated robbery,

"Trial soon.

"Thanks for the salad; I'll take the rest to my room; there's a fridge..

"And, yeah, guys like my legs."

[mid July 2015]

## Red Smudges

Before my uncle married, and immediately began to ignore my aunt,

He dated nightly, many local women, married and unmarried.

We'd find the women's lipstick-stained cigarette stubs in the

Car and pickup ashtrays.

We never emptied those incomplete receptacles.

Now I like to see her lipstick half-circled wine glass

When I start morning coffee.

Sometimes I wash the thin glass - more often I leave it -

Her night remaining in the wet dawn.

Coffee steaming, glass red, I leave to feel the

Puddle-wet street - light yellow and gray.


[mid May 2013]

**Sisters**

The sisters, warm even on the descent,

Stopped at the waterfall,

Pulled off tops and shorts,

Slipped off shoes,

Left bras and panties on,

And walked into the stream,

Over slippery rocks to the cascading spray

Where they raised their arms, laughed

And shivered under snow-melt strings ....

[late June 2013]

## On Rises

South to the gulf flow brown slow Georgia and Alabama rivers,

Through straight tall pines, green and log-choked swamps ...the north
Florida Panhandle.

And on the bluffs, hills, rises above the rivers, the prisons,

Wire within wire for local, state and federal prisoners,

The north Florida employer.

County by county, work,

And the prisoners, daily bused in from Florida's large cities.

With the guards getting pre- or after-work coffee and donuts from the
Nicaraguan,

She married to a north Florida guard.

The prisoners get their powdered eggs and diluted coffee and day-old
bread behind wires.

"Here, your coffee and donuts, and I added your pickup's gas."

That's the Nicaraguan speaking.

Within five miles, convenience store staples, and prison fare basics, too.

Reach the gulf, rivers.

Wash us ....

[mid February 2016]

**Start**

A fat mid-summer full moon sat high in the west.

A rooster crowed.

The partera (midwife) neatly and fast delivered the baby boy.

The partera has a bumper sticker: "We help people out!"

So, the five-minute-old baby heard:

The rooster.

Sensed yellow moonlight in the room.

The teen mother shut her eyes.

The teen father, steps from the delivery, dragged on a cigarette, while dawn broke pink in puffy white and blue clouds.

Whiffs of gray smoke reached the baby, mother and partera.

[mid July 2014]

## Blood and Tribes

I was sitting at the table,

Drinking my coffee too fast, as usual.

A lot of talk of grandkids, kids, mothers, fathers.

I kept quiet, little to add.

I walked home in a humid dawn, mosquitoes biting, chiggers nipping.

What am I?

Why the silence in family tales?

Dare I declare:

I find others more interesting, even if superficial.

Caregivers, truck drivers, nurses, clerks, ag workers.

That's simply me, and comfortable to a point.

***

The Montana motorcyclist.

"Hate helmets, and they're not required in Montana."

A pack of unfiltered Camels in his shirt pocket, gray stubble face lined.

Maybe I'll tell the family centered coffee drinkers about the Montana freedom lover.

But I probably won't, not in their circles.

[late March 2016]

## Blanket

A blanket, the first usually in October in South Texas.

She gets up and goes to a closet.

She returns with a fuzzy blanket, American Indian design lines.

She bought it at a border second-hand shop.

I wonder how many people, now dead, it covered.

Once I loaned an old man a pair of brown socks.

He died in a boarding house room next to mine.

He was carried out in a black rubber sack.

Maybe he had my socks on.

I never got them back.

[mid November 2013]

*The Run of Days*

◇◇◇◇◇◇◇◇◇◇◇◇◇◇◇◇◇◇

French novelist Gustave Flaubert said "To find something interesting, you merely have to look at it long enough." Gene has long had his careful, deeply contemplative eye trained on every element in and around him – neighbors, strangers (of whom there are probably none, in Gene's compassionate world), rivers, couches pitched into alleyways, cups of coffee,  memory, his own heart in his body, and the hearts of his ancestors before him. Everything is interesting. Everything holds weight and measure, but immeasurable significance and possibility. Things feel connected, not flung willy-nilly into view. Time and change are resonant threads of awareness – how perspective shifts depending on age, which side of the river you started out on, the often-invisible quirks of privilege. Gene has room for the grief and the wound. He would heal if he could. When he speaks of "the luxury to write of dormancy" he does so out of humility, but a true observer is never dormant, always engaged. Gene makes the most of every day because it never passes him unawares. His perception is a gift. Invisibly, secretly, offered up to all community… He is also, as a reader quickly notices, the King of the Ellipse…that mysterious ongoing openness which has found a true home in his writings. The run of the days continues. He will be paying attention…

Naomi Shihab Nye

## Straight Tie

...wonder if the tidy man with the

flowered shirt, always pressed,

and also-pressed slacks, shined black shoes,

in his brown jacket, scarf around neck,

red tie lined and centered,

saw Venus break in black eastern clouds,

in gray light, while he walked to his deep corner table for coffee,

after the ice storm dripped away ....

[late January 2014]

## Through Flowers

We used to throw out dead flowers:

Seeds, stems, fragments ...browned, desiccated ....

All, roadside wildflowers.

Now, we leave them in their vases.

Scattered scraps mount on tables ....

We've slowed.

We continue to cut and pick.

We arrange.

We place, adjust, and drop in water-filled vases.

We look daily.

We see them die.

We know.

[mid August 2017]

## Up and Down the Hilly Road
### (In Central Maine)

Bagels with tomatoes and basil on yoghurt.

Bear claw creamy Danish with soda.

Soft bicycles' whoosh.

Soft sandals' slide.

Eight-cylinder pickups' busted muffler roar.

Logging boots' stomp.

Donuts dipped in environmentally acceptable coffee.

Donuts spread under trees - black bear bait.

Merely up and down the same hilly road.

[early September 2016]

**Daylight Savings Ends**

Did the cat know the clocks had been turned back?

It stalked birds rested on ATM machines.

One bird lingered.

The cat pounced.

The sun was higher.

[early November 2019]

## Dormancy

Not as I imagined the end.

I saw myself fighting:

Franco in Spain.

The Whites in Russia.

Bautista in Cuba.

Nazis in Eastern Europe.

Colonists ,,,all over the for-the-taking planet.

Not to be.

Causes in books.

Born wrong and safe.

But staring out a foggy window in McDonald's.

Lights on the roads.

The hunched old sit and stand,

And I approach that state .....

Farm workers, prison guards, caregivers .....

Coffee, sausages, a break ......

Young students, worn parents, less-worn grandparents .....

TV news, bland music, yellow light,

Black-clad workers,

Meaty odors ....

Traffic increases, dawn breaks to light ....

"I'll take a half cup regular, drop of cream."

I have moved into another day,

And if dormant, there is life ...,.

Medical inventions at work  .....

The luxury to write of dormancy,

Reflect,

Think it's time to shave, gray stubble, glasses dirty .....

No, it's not what I imagined ....

[late January 2018]

## Sound Of Silence

At 5:22 a.m., dawn off, and Mercury possible,

"Sound Of Silence" blares from a parked-at-light car.

Contradictory, silence a cover,

Song seeks such, and also crushes ....

***

A lone white chicken lays an egg on a parched lawn in all-in-beds-asleep block.

Music and words well up the street, to the highway.

The fowl, alert to skunks, possums, dogs, cats,

Walks up a brown grassy alley ....

[early July 2016]

## Couch

"Recall when we'd see a couch in an alley?

We'd tip it, shake out the roaches and load it in the car.

To home, same for tables and chairs.

Now we drive past, shake our heads."

You pass on the question and ask, "Wonder who'd put that piece of crap out there?"

I'm quiet.

No need to reconstruct our apartment-filled-with-salvage-things' life of decades back.

I change the topic.

"Wonder if all those people in nursing homes around here know when it's a holiday,

Christmas, Thanksgiving, Fourth of July?

All sorts of decorations on those days in front, the hallways, dining room."

"How do I know?

You know some people in those homes.

Go ask them."

On the same drive, with the sun up,

An all-night party finally ending, bodies swaying, music on.

"I'd call the cops if I lived nearby," you say.

"Come on! You did the same, just like you never passed up thrown-out furniture. Stop blotting so damn much."

"Ok, Ok, enough."

[early July 2014]

## I Did

...and curled into my sleeping bag in the pine forest near the east west road in Colorado ….

...year summer of 1959, the American Road ….

...awoke in a freezing dawn, hitched to a resort town,

...washed dishes, listened to folk music, fumbled with women who knew ….

Now, move the weekly trash bin, water new plants, check the doctors' appointments ….

...ponder how elderly morphs to aged ….

...also, consider that memory is more acute than now ….

So, roll the sleeping bag, shake off sleep, find the road ….

Yes, the trash bin mounts, dishes pile ….

[early December 2019]

# Limping

...to cars and pickups parked in handicap pharmacy slots,

They limp, canes clicking on concrete,

Pills in bottles in white bags.

Toss them onto the passenger's seat,

Climb up - hard - into the driver's seat.

Engine on, roll down the window, cough, then spit phlegm to the concrete ....

Home, and rest, and back soon, maybe the next day ....

Pass on the maybe - for sure to return and return, until ....

[late September 2018]

## Another Day, Hour

"See, she knows me," the pharmacy customer says.

"That's how it is when you age," she adds.

The pharmacists and technicians know me, too.

They don't ask my name or date of birth.

They go directly to the shelves where the filled prescriptions wait.

***

And the last house painting.

And the last car.

And the last bike.

And the last long trip.

And the last bus, its road heard around the curve, the bus not seen, yet,

No stop for me ....

***

How self indulgent.

Central Americans, Africans and Cubans wait "across,"

Waiting for their asylum number to be called ....

And the numbers, so many angles to them ....

Pay, fast track, ahead,

Don't pay, wait in the humidity, trash and vehicle fumes ....

Lives on hold ....

***

Back to the pharmacy,

Was a drug store ....

My options,

Time to play the past, present, future ....

Time to select the best coffee,

The best place,

The best table ....

***

...that river,

Green brown swirling turbulent,

Vegetation spinning,

High fast water ....

[late June 2019]

## Fog Movement

Yes, there are street cats in the fog.

Black-furred bodies walking.

Yes, the homeless unwrap their blankets and start their coin search.

A stench of bathlessness, rotted clothes.

And there are trucks.

Food delivery trucks.

Garbage trucks.

And the crisscrossing car lights, paper delivery car,

Side to side, paper thrown to yards ....

The fog covers dawn, and the vehicles drive away ....

[mid January 2019]

## Two Grapefruit

Thought I had them all,

Ladder to the top,

Arms scratched,

Eyes poked,

Hundreds of grapefruit pulled in early winter.

Painful, itchy work.

But in mid spring I found two more:

One hidden fat round high in green leaves among tiny new fruit,

The other fat round in thick weeds below.

I knocked the high one off with a broom.

It fell heavily to the ground;

I picked it up.

I lifted the other from the weeds.

The two, still good?

Yes, juicy, very juicy ,,,,

[late April 2014]

## Lying There

The heart,

4:32 in the yet-to-come dawn.

Soft lightning.

Muted thunder.

Varied winds.

The storm, gentle.

Heart.

Weak hearts on my mother's side.

Better odds on my father's.

Grandfather, he who ruined a Ford when he hit the brakes and milk cans spilled.

Dead abed, with Spring surrounding.

Mother, who gave up translating, art, music and a lit city for a dark farm.

Dead abed, Summer in its middle.

Now, and the storm powers.

Sharper lightning,

Booms in  clouds,

Wind speeds.

I think heart,

Hear mine,

Feel mine,

Ready ... that  heritage brings me to their bedsides ,,,,


92


[early May 2017]

*Epiphanies*

◇◇◇◇◇◇◇◇◇◇◇◇◇◇◇◇◇◇◇

Writers are a curious lot.

They are driven by their curiosity. They want to know everything they can about their world and they want to understand; they write to find answers. They use language to attempt to come to terms with what they see and hear and feel as they interact with this amazingly complex, so often disruptive and disturbing place we have come to accept as the world we inhabit. How else to understand who we really are in relationship to that immense world that surrounds us?

Gene Novogrodsky is one of us who wants answers to the questions that confront him each and every day he sets off on another early morning walk from his Brownsville home. He is always alert, paying close attention, noticing the smallest pertinent details of both the natural and the human worlds around him – who would notice that a rooster in the alley crowed every seventeen seconds? -- and this accumulation of little things noticed leads him to record later what he has seen, usually in the form of poems or stories. In a single line or phrase he often zeroes in on the very essence of a situation or a problem or a condition. He may surprise both himself and his readers with where his words lead him. In one of his early morning poems, he describes the women who have crossed the bridge from Mexico and are lined up outside the clinic where they will sell their blood. This one quick pan of the camera captures an image that is immediately so powerful and disturbing that I have been haunted by it since I first read it. Good writing does this.

GLEN SORESTAD

95

# Wild Olive White

They arrived in a day, maybe two;

The wild olive white blossoms.

Coating yards, fields and streets.

Wind of all direction flutters them.

Coating moved ....

[mid April 2020 ]

## And Now

The decades,

And the now.

Would you meet now?

Would your eyes meet?

No, the concrete set long ago,

Then, cracked ....

Tiny weeds, thin grasses reach for sun ....

[late July 2017]

# The Poets See

The poets find new grass blades in a cracked sidewalk in mid-March, slush surrounding.

The poets find two garbage collectors waiting for two businesswomen and one businessman to step past.

The poets' eyes see.

The poets' minds warp.

[early February 2015]

## Same Planet (Slight Variations)

Missiles.

Sudan.

Chopin.

[early April 2017]

## Downtown In Late April

"Eat shit and die!" the dope-smoking concrete crew would yell at grumps.

I didn't yell, but I knew how the well-dressed folk on sidewalks and in new cars viewed us: grubby, dirty, dopers ...doing the filthy muddy work for their $250,000 homes' foundations ....

...fished for perch in the Connecticut River as ice went out and dawn broke ....

... love snow-forced deserted streets, and now virus-forced deserted streets, all so still, quiet, rare cats, rare birds, homeless with last night's free food, homeless arranging the cardboard slabs they slept on ....


***


Two black women from Chicago, back from a Mexican dentist/now off to a friend's for breakfast before flying back to Chicago/elementary friends to this day/one a counselor/one an office manager ....

"We met Mexicans in South Side Chicago, and stayed friends," one explains.

They need a cab.

They'd prefer an Uber, but none at this hazy muggy cloying pasty dawn.

"Don't worry! I'll get one; I'll yell for it, like in the movies."

And I do.

"Hey cab! Right here!"

The cab turns, and we negotiate, they in English, I in Spanish.

They get in and off they go.

Maybe they saw this old white man as sincere; who knows in this World, in this United States?

I missed them, even with our but 10 minutes together ....

Hope for a multi-racial, mixed language, mixed gender, mixed social class United States ...?

***

She's on a street corner.

She tries to get cellphone reception.

I walk several blocks with her, and Wi-Fi kicks in.

"I left the guy, just wanted to be free," she says.

She wants to get to her cousins in the western part of the city where she is staying.

Her four kids are with their dad.

"No chance we'll get back together. I have a boyfriend now.

"The kids are doing well in school.

"I've been late with my taxes, same for my unemployment claims from the call center where I worked until the virus."

She'd prefer a cab, but has no money.

Her cousins lack a car and money.

I urge the bus upon her, and tell her where to get off.

I give her a crumpled dollar.

...various jobs, after success in the junior college: computer skills; medical assistant skills.

"I worked at the county jail two years, in the pharmacy.

"All the inmates wanted drugs."

Then she added:

"The boyfriend is in federal prison, drug case.

"We hope the virus will get him out."

She sits on the bus station bench, and waits.

I leave, and cry back: "Get that bus and be sure to tell the driver where you want to get off."

"Thanks."

***

Is that enough?

The homeless eat; their cardboard is in order.

The plasma sellers have already gotten their money, and others line up.

***

Heat builds, and it is only late April.

At least four hot months, and maybe some hurricane-brought rain.

***

Chicago women.

Have a safe flight.

Local woman.

Get some sleep, and do that paperwork;  you have decades to live and grow and be at only 31 ….

The tattoos, blue purple and black, they work ….

[late-April 2020]

## Alley

A ripped sofa, stuffing and wood protruding.

A mattress box spring, busted wires.

A mattress, yellow and brown stained.

A rooster inside a gate, a crow every 17 seconds.

One empty Pepsi can.

The alley, puddles dry.

The street at the end.

[early December 2017]

**Tears, Unexplained**

Why do I cry at music?

No, not always, but enough to wonder.

I offer a reason, which might come close to an explanation.

Could be place, maps, names, air ....

***

The huapango three-man groups move hundreds of stomping feet

In Xilitla, San Luis Potosi, Mexico.

Misty hills, gray clouds, high voices and screeching violins.

Off mountain farms, into town to shop and dance,

Those who aren't "across" in the United States.

They dance.

They bang.

They sweat.

Rain nears.

And I cry.

***

Hundreds of cars and trailer trucks on
The Marine Atlantic ferry dock in North Sydney, Nova Scotia, Canada.

The ferry rocks in blue water,

Sun bright.

Quebec and New Brunswick French couples are off to Newfoundland Labrador.

A military reunion.

I ask a woman to slap a French accordion and fiddle CD into her tape deck.

She does.

I start to dance.

So do the men and women.

The reunion, many dead in Canada's wars.

And I cry.

***

A cool Friday twilight in an old church,

Harbor Grace, Newfoundland Labrador,

Choppy bay water down a hill east,

Shrimp and crab boats secured,

Monthly music night,

All performers welcome.

Newfoundlanders rich with oil money back from Alberta.

They're restless.

The old - their relations - stay hours.

"Foggy Foggy Day" is sung repeatedly.

Away and missing.

And I cry.

***

A cold fog in Spaniard's Bay, Newfoundland Labrador,

On a hill, "Lassy Days, " called such from the molasses paid

Loggers and fishermen a century back.
Dead-at-sea and lost-love Newfoundland ballads,

Irish accents blend off the stage,

Greeley's Reel, a hard-driving band.

Arms linked, I dance with back-home-now Newfoundland women.

"Wonderful," one says, "We're having a time, 'a jig and a reel.'"

And I cry.

***

French and English tents at the Newfoundland Labrador Folk Festival -

Steep hills above St. John's harbor.

Each tent, a fiddle, a voice, a tale.

Rain and wind a day.

Sun the next.

Words words, the past.

And I cry, and I cry  - tent to tent.

***

Port aux Basques, Newfoundland Labrador,

Another ferry rocks in a sunset.

A three-man group plays "Foggy Foggy Day,"

My request.

Passengers, no boarding yet, stop listen.

Night settles.

And I cry.

***

Back stage at a northern Mexico theatre,

I hug sweaty Mexican rocker Jamie Lopez,

His all-over voice,

His killer guitar.

Moved fans line up,

Lyrics of sexual hope in Mexico's hardness.

And I cry.

***

Nothing new these tears,

A North Carolina black church in mountain rain,

Fifty years ago ....

What sounds await ....

[mid September 2010]

## Independence

Can a sunrise move one, even if above a shopping center,

Its pink white yellow, with fading planets and a star high …?

Does it matter there?

Must it be a desert?



[April 30, 2020]

## Unwelcoming Prudence

I used to walk into yards:

On treed bluffs above the Mississippi in Missouri,

On grassy prairies above the Mississippi in Illinois,

In soaked rice fields, levee-protected, near the Mississippi in Arkansas,

On beet-planted plains bordering the Red in North Dakota.

"Some water, please?"

"Sure, help yourself."

Not as certain, not as confident now:

The loaded rifles, shotguns, pistols.

The brown pit bulls on rusted chains.

Fortified islands.

Pass on.

[mid April 2013]

## Ineptitude Slotted

I am seeing my universe.

Maybe.

But it's unsatisfactory, tawdry, hollow, a wisp ....

The plumber splices a line.

He tells me to turn off the water.

I do.

The carpenter tells me to help lift a couch out of his workspace.

I do.

Two simple jobs.

I return to my crumpled vision,

Telling myself my books are my soul - delusion -

As I wanted to do more, be more

Than a stumbling senior who turns off water and lifts a couch ....

[early February 2015]

## To Seed

Cloying heat enters,

A door is open.

Rich soft and dark green

Lettuce, dill and mustard

Bolt to seed.

Leaves and stalks bitter -

Thin reeds of yellow seed crown.

The heat sets its blanket.

[early April 2013]

## Orange In the West

Just before the bus's yellow interior lights dimmed

He told me that his former restaurant boss

Still comes downtown to play scratch lottery tickets.

Urban renewal took the restaurant, and the worker's job.

The bus started west,

Past closing stores,

Around parked cars and trucks.

An orange sunset screened the west,

Black utility poles climbed into twilight,

Flat dark roofs set firm.

A beep, a stop, those yellow lights on,

A passenger off,

Then, lights off.

A soft trip, a sweet shell ....

[mid November 2014]

## Smell

...cigarette from early morning car to work ....

...possum crap on roadside ....

...dead cat in middle of street ....

...humid mist ....

...car exhaust

Blend in the dawn.

Blend in the fog.

Blend in the stillness.

[early April 2019]

## Crow Feather

...taxes, property values,

Sell, buy, repair ....

Goldenrod yellow full.

Black crow feather.

Later dawn.

Earlier dusk.

Owl screech.

Loon cry.

[early August 2019]

# Vulnerability

A heavy cough,

It thickens.

A gum abscess.

It festers, grows.

The cough, a week later, softens.

The abscess, two weeks later, shrinks.

But vulnerability's notch in life's stick has deepened.

[late May 2014]

*For Gene*

## POET FRIENDS

Strange to read you "on" me.
But  I'm" vain enough to like what I "see" in me.
I hope I can inspire more poems.

GENE NOVOGRODSKY

# Gene's Last Game

on the last day
before the end of the world
Gene sits in the bleachers
with no one else
and watches lithe innings
of a high school baseball game
on a scruffy field

and yes, there is no end to this game
they could foul off balls
forever
there is no clock between pitches
no breaks for commercials

the players are young enough
to know that they will live
forever

the bases frayed, the chalk lines dusted over
the ump, the father of one of the players
uniforms sweaty and stained

Gene is delighted with the game
the sun, the afternoon, the joy they play with
and the way time has settled down
quiet in the corners of the diamond.


-- JIM LAVILLA-HAVELIN

# Somewhere Along the Border Line

*Something there is that doesn't love a wall.*
*That wants it down.*         *Robert Frost*


A friend of mine lives near the Rio Grande,
a Texas border town, and is a dawn walker,
unsurprised on his strolls to meet migrants,
witness their attempts to become invisible.
Sanctuary-seekers, they have survived
unimagined woes and evils through a land
beset with drugs, stained with blood:
those who kill to supply them, those who
kill to get them – between them, the unfortunates.
The survivors who reach here have endured,
aliens arrived in Eden, seeking a meal,
or even a windfallen fruit.

Those who share his feelings know
the stark, high wall, quick-triggered guards,
keen-nosed dogs, overhead drones and copters,
searchlights, deadly bullets, ceaseless patrols --
all conditions he believes wrong-headed
in his country, counter to those American
ideals he has always cherished.

Early morning border-crossers, desperation
locked away in strongbox faces, seek
only what each and all of us want --
a safe place to rest at day's end.


-- **GLEN SORESTAD**

# Poem for Miriam Rodriguez
*for Gene Novogrodsky*

I knew nothing of this woman, until I read
your poem. My country is not without
its own victimized and murdered women.

You did not personally know Miriam.
But I can understand how what you learned
fired your rage and sorrow into powerful lines.

That a brave woman should be assassinated,
in her Tamaulipas home in a fusillade of bullets
because she dared to speak -- dared to spite those

who demanded her silence. Freedom of speech
in cartel-drugged Mexico, where the value
of a single life is low, comes at a high premium.

For every Miriam Rodriguez there is a poem
about courage and its cost; with each reading,
each utterance, she dies, again and again.

-- GLEN SORESTAD

# Afternoon of Gifts

Intruding on talk about baseball memories
and Mexican cartel-flavored bus adventures
and Grossman's novel on damaged
Israelis and their Muslim shadows,
the polite eavesdropper speaks
of his Palestinian girlfriend, born
in Kuwait, medically trained in Latvia,
aiming to immigrate to Canada,
while he, ex-Marine, will soon
return to lucrative contract work
in Afghanistan or Iraq. He pulls
out a handcrafted souvenir, a metal
keychain missing its keys,
a faceless form joined to the daggered
landscape of Israel, Arabic lettering
along one side, and gives it
as a memento to our chance exchange
in a Texas border coffee shop,
center of a narrowing universe.

-- CHIP DAMERON

# Last Mail Run

Postman got in early, put the single
postcard in his leather bag,
left before the others arrived
to mark the prefabricated funeral.

Last day of September. After, no more
bills, letters, circulars—everything
electrified or short-circuited,
will of the people's chosen surrogates.

He parked at one end, walked again
the familiar route, touching the tip
of his pith helmet to passing cars,
sweating out his ticking memories.

Last block, next to last house,
he handed the card to the woman
who stepped down from her porch,
thanked him, read the card, smiled.

He watched her clothespin the card
to the last gap in the line stretching
from post to tree limb, postcards
fluttering like Tibetan prayer flags.

He walked away, remembering
G.N.'s handwritten message: *Early
light, quiet moon fading. Every leaf
of your oak is another word now. Paz.*


-- Chip Dameron

# Mr. Novo

Former students write from prison,
read the books you send by mail.

Others sit in their cells, parsing
their sentences, killing time.

Some are in med school, remember
the ethics of stories, of discussions.

Others checked off your box, consider
which specialties bring more bucks.

That waitress talks about her baby,
her sick father across, takes your order.

Those two wave as you bike by,
sweating, and call out their names.

you took them all at face value,
accepted what they gave back.

They've taken whatever they would.
At dawn you walk the neighborhood.

-- CHIP DAMERON

## Rambling Stories

As we walked one winter morning
through your neighborhood and took
the new hike and bike trail
toward downtown, we soon found
ourselves on a country road
in Ireland, hearing McGahern's people
repeat close-held prejudices amidst
the evidence of change, and then
we hiked up a mountain village
in Gage's northwest Greece and hid
in a cave, the Nazis now gone
but teenage boys and girls forced
into comradeship, andartes and
andartinas sent to stop the royalists'
bullets, and next we walked along
a wet street in the Istanbul dark,
holding an unfamiliar object that
might be a clue to another of Pamuk's
Byzantine mysteries, but before
we could establish its talismanic
meaning we had reached our destination,
a small downtown café, and as Larry
the owner refilled our coffee cups
he told us stories of his days
in the merchant marine, his childhood
in rural western North Carolina,
his string of wives, his ninth grade
education, his thirst for books, and
his town's intolerance toward outsiders—
we'd send a couple of the boys
to kick their butts—and he smiled
as he looked across the counter
at his Mexican wife and ticked off

successes of children and step-children
in this border town that has taken
him in and let him talk and talk.


-- **CHIP DAMERON**

## Somewhere in Maine

Late summer: early morning
loggers roll in, fill the air
with angry growls, excise
towering cabin crushers

the visiting resident inside
slices baseball memories

Portland Sea Dogs and
Altoona Curve yesterday,
Yankees and Senators
seventy-one years ago

even the leaves left behind
have a season to remember

-- CHIP DAMERON

# End of the Rio Grande

We parked at the end of the road,
last stop in South Texas, and walked
an hour in the early light, the sea
a bountiful blue, the brown pelicans
patrolling overhead, the day promising
clean heat and clear lines of sight.

Ahead, a lone green and white van
marked one side of the river, or so
it seemed, the white sand it guarded
no different than the sand a yard
farther on. We could just make out,
a hundred yards to the west, the last
glint of the drought-deadened river.

Standing in the parched river bed
were a man on this side, a woman
and a baby on the other, their words
muffled by the laughing gulls' cries,
another border story, another dry day,
the waves rolling in, rolling in.

-- CHIP DAMERON

# December Walk with Gene

We left your house
before sunrise, streets wet
with a rare misting.

Striding into downtown traffic,
talking about books again,
passing men wanting work.

Café breakfast, spacious station
for buses—now open,
royal palms rising nearby.

Brief stops for chats:
articulate electrician's boyhood
passion for broken appliances,

city planner at a keyshop,
mechanic near a meat market,
frail lady gathering litter.

Voice of the neighborhood,
leading by bamboo staff,
you thumped us homeward.

-- **CHIP DAMERON**

# ABOUT THE AUTHOR

Eugene "Gene" Novogrodsky has lived in Brownsville, Texas more than 32 years. He writes slices that reach from Mexico, through The United States and into Canada. He is a founder of the Narciso Martinez Cultural Arts Center Writers Forum in San Benito, Texas. He now writes and reads with ad hoc groups in Brownsville.

Life's plate has endless food for him.